In The Beginning

Bible Study on the Book of Genesis

By

Ricky LaVaughn

LaVauri Publishing House

In The Beginning:
Bible Study on the Book of Genesis
Copyright 2009 by Elder Ricky LaVaughn

Published by LaVauri Publishing House
Printed in the United States of America
www.lavauri.com

Other Books by Ricky LaVaughn

Foundation of the Fire
When Roses Cry

Cover by: Ricky LaVaughn

Acknowledgments

First and foremost, I have to thank God for an opportunity to serve Him by putting together this study. Also, to all those who where a part of this Bible Study when we gleaned through the book of Genesis, it was great studying with you.

Here are a few links where you can read the Bible Online.

http://www.biblegateway.com/

http://www.onlinebible.net/

http://www.bible.com/

http://www.blueletterbible.org/

http://www.allonlinebible.com/

http://www.seventhday.org/

http://bible.logos.com

The book of Genesis is essential for people because of it's wealth of knowledge and testimony to the people God lead. It spans the greatest amount of time when compare to any other books of the Bible, yet it gets very personal with the Lord's dealing in people's lives.

In The Beginning, was chosen as a title because it is the first words of Genesis and the Bible. It allows us to realize that here is the start. This is where we see the initial set up of our world, and the Authority of God. We often question God and his true ruler of this world. However, we must realize that God has set up everything, and all things belong to Him.

Look over the people that we will study and realize that they're not perfect. Yet they still had a desire to do God's will and fulfill His promise. You are not an accident; the Lord has a mission for you. Remember that just like the people in Genesis, you may not be perfect, but do not allow that to stop you from doing what God has said, giving Him the glory with your life.

Each lesson in this Bible Study is broken into two sections.

1.) The first part are questions that stems from the chapters we will cover in Genesis. Look at the top of each lesson to see what chapters we will cover for that lesson. It is good to read the chapters first then go to the lesson; however, you can read the chapters as you answer the questions as well.

2.) Personal Study: these questions deal with building a personal relationship by taking the lessons we learn from each section. They sometimes cover events in the character's lives as well as applying your own personal feelings and actions to their situation. The thing here is to be honest and really look at the lessons that Genesis can teach us.

Just remember this book was meant to be written in, so take notes and have fun building a relationship with God.

Table of Contents

LESSON 1

Genesis 1 – 2

The Creation Of The World And Humankind

1)   Describe the Earth when God set out to create it?

Genesis 1:1-2, Jeremiah 4:22-23

2)   Next to each day, write a few things that God created.

1st day: **Genesis 1:3-5** _____

2nd day: **Genesis 1:6-8** _____

3rd day: **Genesis1:9-13** _____

4th day: **Genesis1:14-19** _____

5th day: **Genesis 1:20-23** _____

6th day: **Genesis 1:24-31** _____

7th day: **Genesis 2:1-3** _____

3)   What method does God use to bring creation into being?

Genesis 1:3, 6, 9, 14, 20, 24

4)   What does the Bible say at the end of each day to give us a timeline on how long creation took?

Genesis 1:5, 8, 13, 19, 23, 31

5)   Chapter 2:1-3 is actually a continuation of chapter one. Why is rest important and what should we do to honor God on that day?

Genesis 2:1-3, Exodus 20:8-11

Now let's look at the creation of humankind. Between chapters 1 and 2 we get a clear picture at the detail God took to create us.

6)   In whose image are people created?

Genesis 1:26-27, Genesis 2:19-20

7)   All other created beings and things God called into existence. How does the Bible

describe people coming into being?

Genesis 2:7,18,21-23

8)   The Lord set up marriage for people. He also gave the couple a job and some

guidelines. What where they?

Genesis 1:28-29, 2:16-17

9)   What is the Biblical view of a married couple?

Genesis 2:24, Matthew 19:4-6, 1 Corinthians 7:1-5

PERSONAL STUDY

A)   In a world of stress and problems why would it be important to take the time to rest

and reflect on God? How can this help us as a society and individual cope with our

problems?

B)   Notice that marriage was created before sin and that God called them to fill the

Earth. The Lord set up a home (Eden), a job (take care of the animals), and then the

call to fill the Earth. In our lives what are some of the needs that God provides for

His people before and during marriage?

C)   Because there was no one else, why would it be a bad thing for Adam to be alone? In

our life what is something we can do single and things we can do in marriage?

D)   The Bible looks at a marriage as a joining of two people. This means both partners represent each other. They become one in that if one hurt so does the other. If one is happy then both are happy. Even in our society, we make it against the law to incriminate oneself. This means that married couples cannot be forced to testify against your spouse. Knowing all of this, how should we treat each other in marriage? If a person is single what steps can they take to prepare themselves for marriage.

F)   Knowing you are created and not formed by accident, what is your purpose in this world? Why are you important for this current society and time?

LESSON 2

Genesis 3

Fall Of Humanity

1)   What was the question posed to Eve that would make her doubt God?

Genesis 3:1

2)   What was Eve's response? What did God say to them about the tree?

Genesis 3:2-3, Genesis 2:16-17

3)   How did the serpent appeal to Eve in doubting God's word?

Genesis 3:4-5

4)   Trying to be higher then God is nothing new for Satan. What does the prophet Isaiah

describe Lucifer's sin and character flaw? What will ultimately happened to him?

Isaiah 14:12-19

5)   What was Eve's decision? Did she follow God or believe the serpent? What was

Adam's response?

Genesis 3:6-7

6)   When God walked through the gardens, what was the early couple's response?

Genesis 3:8-11

7)   After God posed the question of eating the forbidden fruit, what did Adam and Eve

      do?

Genesis 3:12-13

8)   What was the punishment for the following beings for bringing sin into the world?

Genesis 3:14-19

Serpent: **Genesis 3:14-15**

Eve: **Genesis 3:16**

Adam: **Genesis 3:17-19**

9)   What was the result of Adam and Eve's sin?

Genesis 3:20-24

PERSONAL STUDY

A)   Notice the progression of sin. First we listen to the benefits of sin, then we see how

its good, after that we reason the benefits of doing the sin, (Genesis 3:1-6.) Give an

example of sin following this pattern.

B)   People do not like to take responsibility for their actions. Both Adam and Even

blamed others for their personal choices. Yet both where still punished. What can we

do to take responsibility for our actions even when we are wrong? How would

society be different if all people worldwide took personal responsibility?

C)   Adam and Eve where given the command to not touch one tree, but they disobeyed God. Now there are hundreds of laws and the Devil is all about getting us to break them. What means should we take to keep God's laws and obey His word?

D)   Why would the possibility of temptation be in the Garden of Eden?

E)   What is the fascination to be like gods and to know everything? That's what got Lucifer and ultimately the first people on Earth to turn from the Lord. Do you still see people wanting to be more and more powerful for selfish reason? Why does this ultimately lead to destruction?

F)	Notice in Genesis 3:16 that it states that men would rule over women. Which means God's original plan was a complimentary type of marriage and not one of dominance. How do you still see the effects with ruler ship in a relationship and why would woman have an automatic desire for their husband but men do not have the same for women?

G)	Was the punishment too harsh for Adam and Eve or would they have continued to break more rules?

LESSON 3

Genesis 4 – 6

The Rise Of Evil

1) After Adam and Eve where forced out of the garden, they had two sons. What where their name and what jobs did they have?

Genesis 4:1-2

2) Between the two brothers, whose offering did God respect?

Genesis 4:3-5

3) The Lord warned Cain of the malice in his heart. What was Cain's reaction to his brother because God did not accept his gifts?

Genesis 4:6-8

4) The Lord is clear on what is right and acceptable and what is not. Often we like to bring whatever we want, like Cain, and expect God to take it. What did Jesus say about those who believe they're on the right but is wrong?

Matthew 7:21-23

5) What was Cain's curse for killing his brother?

Genesis 4:9-15

Genesis 4:16 through 5:32 is the genealogy of Cain and Seth. Seth became the next son to replace Able. Clearly as time progressed, Adam and Eve had more children and this helped populate the Earth. Read the genealogy to understanding growth and population of the world.

6) Within the genealogy a person is mentioned to have a very special relationship with God. Who was he and what happened to him?

Genesis 5:21-24

7)   The period before the flood is referred to as antediluvian. What are the mindset, action, and behavior of the people? How was God going to deal with them?

Genesis 6:1-7

8)   Although God was going to wipe out the Earth, He had a remnant to be saved. Who was he and what was the names of his children?

Genesis 6:8-13, Genesis 5:25-32

9)   What was God's plan for Noah and his family? What did Noah have to do for God?

Genesis 6:14-18

10)   How where the animals to be saved? What other commands did God give Noah?

Genesis 6:19-22

11)   Today, God will save all of those who believe and desire to follow Him. Describe what will take place, past and present to those who have a relationship with Him. How does this bring you comfort with any love ones you have lost?

1 Thessalonians 4:13-18

PERSONAL STUDY

A)   Enoch was an incredible person who talked and walked with God constantly. Remember he was living in a world full of sin but was married and had children. Through all of these responsibilities and problems from the world, he still had a close/personal relationship with God. Is a relationship like this possible in today's society? What steps can a person take to make that happen?

B)   Notice the Earth in Noah's time (Genesis 6:5, 11-12). The people had corrupt ways, constantly thinking evil, and violent. How is this similar to our world? Noah and his family were all that survived the flood. Is your family, like Noah, ready to follow God's command?

C)   What in your life are you assuming that God does not care or require you to do but in reality does?

LESSON 4

Genesis 7 – 8

The Flood

1)   The Lord made a difference between clean and unclean animals. How many of each

       was Noah ordered to take and why?

Genesis 7:1-3

2)   What was God's plan for the Earth and how long was it going to last?

Genesis 7:4

3)   What did Noah do with God's request? How long did it take before the rain fell once

       the family and animals where on the ark?

Genesis 7:5-10

4)   Describe the flood and destruction. Take notice of how long the flood remained.

Genesis 7:11-24

5)   When did the ark rest and on what mountain? Also what month did the water come

down to see tops of the mountain?

Genesis 8:1-5

6)   Noah sent out birds from the ark while the water was subsiding. Why did he do this,

what where the birds, and what happened?

Genesis 8:6-12

7)   When did the people and animals leave the ark?

Genesis 8:13-19

8)   What did Noah do upon leaving the ark and what was God's response?

Genesis 8:20-22

PERSONAL STUDY

A) When having animals enter the ark the Lord makes a difference between clean and unclean. Read Leviticus 11 to see what animals where allowed to be eaten and which ones where not. Why would God make a difference in what we eat?

B) There was a week in the boat before the rain started, (Genesis 7:10). What must have been the mindset of Noah? Remember that others can see the boat so he was probably being jeered for making it.

C) Noah had to wait a long time in the boat but believed that God would do what He said. In your life what is a promise you're waiting for? Do you still believe even if others around you doubt God's favor in your life?

D)   Notice that Noah worshipped God for deliverance from the flood. When God
       delivers you from a terrible situation why is it important to praise and worship Him
       for what He has done in your life?

E)   Now it is just Noah and his family. Loneliness would set in had it not been for the
       Lord. God is here with you all the time, what steps do you take to remember that
       you're never alone and that God is with you all the time.

Matthew 28:18-20

LESSON 5

Genesis 9 – 11:9

The Aftermath And Rebellion

1)   What rules did God make for Noah and his family?

Genesis 9:1-7

2)   Re-read verses 1 and 7 of Genesis chapter 9. Why is there particular importance

made on this subject?

3)   What is the covenant that God makes to every living thing on the Earth and what is

the symbol?

Genesis 9:8-17

4)   Describe what happened to Noah and the conflict between him, his sons, and the

grandsons.

Genesis 9:18-27

5)   How long did Noah live after the flood and what age did he died?

Genesis 9:28-29

Chapter ten of Genesis is a generation list of the three sons. Take notice of their names and the nations that will come from them. Many will show up in various parts of the Bible.

6)   Describe the people after the flood. What did they do that showed their mistrust of God?

Genesis 11:1-4, Genesis 9:1,7,11

7)   What did the Lord do to the people for their rebellion?

Genesis 11:5-9

PERSONAL STUDY

A)   Ham's son was cursed for Ham's sin of looking at his dad in a bad way. In what

ways have the choices of our ancestors effect us today? Also, how can our decisions

effect future generations?

B)   Should Noah take responsibility for his drunken behavior? Explain.

C)   God clearly told the people to repopulate the earth and that He will not destroy the

world. By building the tower they disobeyed both commands. In our society do we

live our lives by disobeying God? How do we do this and what ways can we stop?

D)   In the scripture "let us make a name" also meant the people declaring dominance

over oneself. Often the naming of something declares the authority you have over

something else. How would God view the people making their own name and usurp

His authority? Have our society tried to declare our own authority? If so, how?

E)   Communication is the foundation to a powerful society as well as a personal relationship. Notice when God confused the language the tower construction stopped. What ways is communication used to bridge the world together? How can this be positive and negative?

F)   On a personal level, what communication techniques can you do to build a relationship with family, friends, co-workers, spouse, etc.

LESSON 6

Genesis 11:10 – 12

The Man Called Abram

1)   Abraham came through the family line of Shem. Read **Genesis 11:10-25**, for the generational line and look at the chart. What do you notice about the lifespan with each passing generation? In what ways is this fulfilling prophecy of God's command before the flood?

Genesis 6:3,5

Father	Son	Age when Father had Son	Years they lived
Shem	Arphaxad	100	600
Arphaxad	Salah	35	438
Salah	Eber	30	433
Eber	Peleg	34	434
Peleg	Reu	30	239
Reu	Serug	32	239
Serug	Nahor	30	230
Nahor	Terah	29	148

Terah	Abram, Nahor, Haran
Haran	Lot

Abram is Lot's Uncle.

2)   Read **Genesis 11:26-32** and describe Abram's family line as well as who they

married and where they lived.

3)   What did God tell Abram to do and what was His promise for the patriarch?

Genesis 12:1-3

4)   How old was Abram when he obeyed and who did he take? Was Abram supposed to

take everyone he did, look at verse 1 of Genesis 12?

Genesis 12:4-6

5)   God revisited Abram to assure him of His plan for the patriarch. What was it and

what disaster happened that could have shook Abram's trust?

Genesis 12:7-10

6)   Describe what happens when Abram went into Egypt. How would you consider

Abram's actions?

Genesis 12:11-16

7) How did God treat the Pharaoh of the land?

Genesis 12:17

8) What was the resolution between Pharaoh and Abram in dealing with Sarai?

Genesis 12:18-20

PERSONAL STUDY

A)   God has given us a 120-year lifespan on Earth because of sin, yet 99.9% of the

population does not get close to that number. What does this say about how far we

have fallen for God's plan and what steps should we take to ensure longevity?

B)   There's something that God cannot do. What is it and how does this affect your

faith?

Numbers 23:19, Titus 1:2, Hebrews 6:18

C)   Abram asked Sarai to tell a half-truth because he was in fear of people instead of

trusting God. Twice before going into Egypt the Lord assured him of a heir. Abram's

disbelief caused panic and pain in the Egyptian household. What have you done that

hurt the promises of God do to disbelief or lack of faith?

D)   Do you feel the Christian church truly believe God or are we going through the

motions?

LESSON 7

Genesis 13 – 14

Rescuing A Family Member

1)   What was Abram's financial status when leaving Egypt and where did he go?

Genesis 13:1-3, Genesis 12:8

2)   What happened between Abram and Lot's servants? What decision was made to end

the problem?

Genesis 13:4-9

3)   Where did Lot choose and what did Abram get? What is good and bad about Lot's

new home?

Genesis 13:10-13

4)   God gave Abram a promise. What was it and what metaphor did God use to explain this promise?

Genesis 13:14-16

5)   What did God tell Abram to do and why? Where did Abram go and what did he do for the Lord?

Genesis 13:17-18

6)   Read **Genesis 14:1-9** and describe who is fighting and why? Due to this conflict, why would this be problematic for Lot?

7)   What happened to Lot during this time of war?

Genesis 14:10-12

8)   When Abram heard of Lot's capture, what did he do?

Genesis 14:13-16

9)   After Abram's victory who met with him? Who did Abram give tithes to and describe this person?

Genesis 14:17-20, Hebrews 7:1-10

10)   What did the King of Sodom offer?

Genesis 14:21

11)   What was Abram's response to the King of Sodom and why? How was this a sign of

respect to God and the earthly King?

Genesis 14:22-24

LaVaughn

PERSONAL STUDY

A)   God believes in blessing His people. Read the scriptures below and write how God

has blessed you, is blessing you, and what blessings are on the way?

3 John 1:2, Matthew 7:7-11, John 1:1-3, Proverbs 10:22, Malachi 3:10

B)   Abram made a difference between the sources of his blessing. How can we apply this

same practice and mindset in our lives? What resources are out there so God can

bless you?

C)   When choosing land, Lot should have given Abram first choice out of respect to his age and authority. Although Abram was nice enough to let Lot choose, still the younger should have given the elder the right of way. What ways have we disrespected our seniors and elderly people? How can we show them respect and do great things for them?

D)   The Bible states the men of Sodom was exceedingly sinful. First, what could that statement mean, and second should Lot of chosen to stay in this city?

E)   Its easy to judge Lot from the information we know now about Sodom. However, if you where given a similar opportunity for your wealth to grow more then you can imagine and many other delights where guaranteed, would you live in a city like Sodom? Are there cities currently that for you would be a place for success but could lead to a personal downfall? For example if fishing takes away valuable family time that would lead to a breakup, would you move to a place that is known as a fishing community?

F)   When looking over your life, are you currently where God wants you to be? Is it time for a change?

LESSON 8

Genesis 15 -16

The Plan For Children

1)   How does God describe Himself to Abram when He speaks to the patriarch?

Genesis 15:1

2)   What solution did Abram have to fulfill God's promise?

Genesis 15:2-3

3)   What was God's response and how did Abram take it? What did the Lord tell him to

do?

Genesis 15:4-12

4)   God lays out the future of Abram's generations. Describe it and the vision that

Abram experienced?

Genesis 15:13-21

5.)   Sometimes when we face a long period of waiting to do something for God we make

mistakes. We believe we have to do something with good intentions but it can ruin

the situation. Look at Sarai's suggestion to Abram. What was it and how can this be

looked upon as desperation?

Genesis 16:1-3

6)   The reality of the decision hit Sarai hard. She knew it was done in error. What did

she do to Hagar?

Genesis 16:4-6

7)   Hagar was nothing more then a pawn in the Abram's and Sarai's plan. God saw her

and was moved with compassion. What was the promise that God told this

handmaid?

Genesis 16:7-12

8)   How old was Abram when the child was born? Now notice when the covenant was

made? With a wait that long, can you understand why they felt like moving on their

time?

Genesis 16:13-16, Genesis 12:1-4

PERSONAL STUDY

A)   Abram leaving his homeland to having a child with Hagar was eleven years. During

this time, Abram had shown when his faith wasn't strong. If you had to wait for such

a long time can you see why they had doubts? Did the mistrust and not having faith

prolong the time of the blessing? Why would Abram be made to wait so long?

B)   What promise or dream did God give you that you have to wait for? During Abram's

journey God showed up to assure Abram that the promise will be fulfilled. What has

God done for you that the promise will be fulfilled in your life?

C)   As you can see in this lesson we often hurry God along by doing things we believe

will help the situation. However, like Abram and Sarai it only makes things worst.

What things have you done to help God along, only for it to be a mistake and cause

problems?

D)   Honestly speaking, if you were in Abram and Sarai's place would you have made the

same decision? Use another example if you know you wouldn't commit this act. For

example take money from someone to give to another unknowingly. Or telling a lie

on someone else so you can get a job that God has promised you. If you know you

can fulfill God's call would you do it by any means possible or by the means that

God has chosen?

E)   Describe Hagar's faith to go back after being kicked out? She knew that she was unwanted yet she listened to God. What does this tell you about her relationship with the Lord?

F)   Currently we are waiting for Christ to return. With the wait being so long, do you see evidence of doubt and laziness in the community, church, and other areas? Do we act like we're waiting for Jesus to come again or do we approach it as some wonderful story to help people deal with the pain of this world?

LESSON 9

Genesis 17 – 18

The Finalization Of The Covenant

1)   The beginning of chapter 17 is when God revealed that within a year the promised child will come. How old was Abram and what was his response?

Genesis 17:1-3

2)   What did God change about Abram and what practice did the Lord institute? What does this symbolize?

Genesis 17:4-10

3)   Who was to go through the (practice) set up by God? What would happen to those who did not?

Genesis 17:11-14

4)   What did God state about Sarai and what was to come from her? How old was she

during this promise?

Genesis 17:15-16

5)   How did Abraham respond and what did he suggest?

Genesis 17:17-18

6)   What was God's response and when was the promise fulfilled?

Genesis 17:19-21

7)   What did Abraham do? How is this a show of faith?

Genesis 17:22-27

8)   When Abraham was greeted by the Lord in the form of three men, what did he do? How is this a show of good hospitality to the guests? Why is there a blessing in this form of help?

Genesis 18:1-8, Hebrews 13:1-3

9)   What did the Lord say that got Sarah to laugh? What was her reasoning and did she take responsibility for her action?

Genesis 18:9-15, Jeremiah 32:17

10)   What did the Lord plan on doing to Sodom upon leaving Abraham? What does Abraham quest for compassion on those citizens?

Genesis 18:16-23

11)   What was the final number Abraham convinced the Lord to spare in Sodom?

Genesis 18:24-33

PERSONAL STUDY

A)   Not how many years it took for the promise to come (Genesis 17:1-3) after Ishmael

        was born (Genesis 16:16). Can you blame Abram for his reaction? How would you

        react if put in a similar situation?

B)   At 99 and 90 years of age, would you believe in having children? Do we forget the

        promise of God if it has been a long time sense the blessing was first pronounced?

C)   Notice before Abraham was to receive the blessing he had to go through some

        changes. Why would this be necessary and what changes can you see that needs to

        take place in your life, city, church, country, etc.

D)   Why would Sarah lie? Are there times we do not take responsibility for our actions?

Why do we do this and does this make the situation better?

E)   In Sodom, a few could have saved many. What does this show about God's

compassion on the wicked as long as His people are present? Read the scriptures

below and detail how God views people and His desire to save them?

Ezekiel 18:20-24, 32; Ezekiel 22:30-31

LESSON 10

Genesis 19

Hell On Earth

1)   At night two angels came to Sodom. Lot saw them and showed great hospitality like

his Uncle Abraham (Genesis 19:1-3). What did the men of Sodom demand of Lot,

which reflects the opposite of Lot's generosity?

Genesis 19:4-5

2)   Amazingly, Lot did not want to give them the strangers but offered something else.

What was it and how did the crowd respond?

Genesis 19:6-9

3)   In other areas of the Bible it list the sins of Sodom. What are some of them and how

was it displayed at Lot's house?

Isaiah 3:8-9, Ezekiel 16:46-50, Proverbs 6:16-19, Leviticus 18:19-23

4)   How was the situation handled?

Genesis 19:10-11

5)   What did the angels order Lot to do? What was the response he received from his

family?

Genesis 19:12-14

6)   Lot could only take his wife and two daughters. How did the angels help them?

Genesis 19:15-16

LaVaughn

7)   What were the orders the angels gave the family?

Genesis 19:17

8)   What city did Lot go to and why? What does this show about his character?

Genesis 19:18-23

9)   What happened to Sodom and Gomorrah? What other people where given as examples for being destroyed or punished due to their behavior?

Genesis 19:24-25, 2 Peter 2:4-9, Jude 1:5-7

10)   What happened to Lot's wife? What command did she disobey?

Genesis 19:26, Genesis 19:17

11)   Abraham was spared from the destruction. He was close enough to see the fire but was not affected. (Genesis 19:27-29) This was not the case of Lot. Although his life and two daughters where spared, what actions happened next? How is their action a testament to living in a city polluted with evil thoughts?

Genesis 19:30-38

PERSONAL STUDY

A)   Remember that God only needed ten people to save the city. Only four was fleeing and three got away with some extra push. Not even Lot's family was enough to save the city. If the following was true today and God decided to destroy your town, are there enough in your family, church, school, job, etc to save the town? Think about the sphere of influence that is needed for many to be saved?

B)   Pride was one of the problems plaguing Sodom. We have to remember that pride is what caused Satan (Lucifer) to be kicked out of Heaven (Isaiah 14:12-17). If pride is such an evil to the Lord then why do we celebrate and promote people because of it? What characteristics does pride have that draws people? Why should we change our behavior and mindset to not have this abomination before God?

C)   Look over question three from this lesson. Does our society display some of the same characteristics? If not with fire how else can a town, neighborhood, and country, be punished by God?

D)   Lot's daughters are classic examples as to what happen when we allow ourselves to be influenced by evil. What are current examples of things influencing us in a negative way and how can we change this?

E)   Lot's wife could not let her home life go. Look around you right now. One day all that you see will be rubble. Are you willing to give it up to go with Christ in Heaven? Is anything holding you to Earth?

LESSON 11

Genesis 20 – 21

The Birth Of A Promise

1)   Where did Abraham go? While there, what did he tell Sarah to say and what happened to her?

Genesis 20:1-2

2)   What did God tell Abimelech and what was the King's response?

Genesis 20:3-7

3)   This event is similar to a previous situation to Abraham. Compare both and why did Abraham tell the King about his connection to Sarah?

Genesis 20:8-11, Genesis 12:9-14

4)   What was Abraham's and Sarah's relationship?

Genesis 20:12

5)   What blessing did Abimelech get for returning Sarah and what did the King get from

        Abraham?

Genesis 20:13-18

6)   What event happened when Abraham was 100 years old? Describe what happened

        during this time and what the two parents did and said.

Genesis 21:1-8

7)   During this time Abraham had to do something he did not want to. What was it and

why did this happen?

Genesis 21:9-14

8)   What happened with Hagar and Ishmael?

Genesis 21:15-21

9)   What matter could have cause strife between Abraham and Abimlech? How did they

handle the situation?

Genesis 21:22-34

PERSONAL STUDY

A)   Abraham had Sarah to tell the partial truth about their relationship. This still caused problems with the King of Gerer. Are partial truths just as bad as a full lie? How does God look at this sin?

B)   You would think with Sarah being pregnant that Abraham would have the faith that God will keep him alive. It's possible that Abraham believed his job was over so he could die and be of no service. What other possible reasons could Abraham have in not showing faith? If put in a similar situation would you have responded the same way?

C)   Sarah was pregnant at ninety years old. Yet she still looked good enough for a king to desire her. What does this say about God blessing His people's physical appearance? Because we are God's representatives should we aspire to look our best? (physical shape, dress, character, etc) What ways can we accomplish this?

D)   Notice the joy from having Isaac displayed by the two parents. When a promise is fulfilled how should we respond?

E)   God was merciful and compassionate on Hagar and Ishmael. He blessed her and kept his lineage to become great. When looking at God's compassion, what does this say about His love for all people, even those who have been cast out by society.

LESSON 12

Genesis 22 – 23

The Test Of Faith

1) What is the request God asked of Abraham?

Genesis 22:1-2

2) How did Abraham respond with actions? What thought does the Bible record was going through his mind?

Genesis 22:3-5, Hebrews 11:17-19

3) Look at the question that Isaac asked Abraham. How do you think that made Abraham feel?

Genesis 22:6-8

4)   Describe the sacrifice and the faith Isaac had to be a part of this event. Also, note the

joy of Abraham hearing the voice of the Angel.

Genesis 22:9-12

5)   What was ultimately waiting for Abraham after his show of faith?

Genesis 22:13-14

6)   Due to Abraham's action what blessing was pronounced on him?

Genesis 22:15-18

Genesis 22:19-24 describe Abraham's extended family having children. Look at Genesis 11:24-32 for a reference.

7)   How old was Sarah when she passed away?

Genesis 23:1-2

8)   Read **Genesis 23:3-20**. Why was it important for Abraham to own the piece of land instead of just receiving it?

PERSONAL STUDY

A)   Before having to sacrifice Isaac, Abraham was given other chances to try his faith. He failed so later was given the ultimate test of the promise. In your life are there tests that you still need to past? What steps can you take to insure victory?

B)   Abraham did not tell Sarah about his plan from God. Sometimes we want to share everything the Lord has told us. Why are there times when we should not?

C) Describe Isaac's faith during this process. Remember that he's listening to his dad so he had to be a willing participant. Isaac easily could have said no and left. However, he didn't. Describe the character show in Isaac?

D) God ultimately provided the sacrifice and the blessing was secure. When waiting on the promise of God what blessing can you gain? How is God getting the glory?

LESSON 13

Genesis 24 – 25:18

The Marriage Of Isaac

1)   What promise did Abraham order his servant to make?

Genesis 24:1-4

2)   The servant proposed a valuable question. What was it and what was Abraham's response?

Genesis 24:5-9

3)   What is the servant's prayer? Look at the details in the prayer. What qualities was the servant looking for when praying to God?

Genesis 24:10-14

4)   Soon as the servant finished, God answered the prayer. Who was she and what did

        she do to show that God answered the prayer?

Genesis 24:15-21

5)   The woman was kindred to Abraham. Who was her father and what is her

        relationship to Abraham and her future husband Isaac?

Genesis 24:22-24, Genesis 22:20-23, Genesis 11:24-29

6)   Rebekah's generosity did not stop at the well. What else did she offer to the servant

        and the group with him?

Genesis 24:25-32

7)   Read **Genesis 24:33-53**, for a recount of the servant's prayer and the blessing he

        received. Why do you believe the Bible would recount the entire passage in such

        detail? What important lessons can we gleam from this story being told twice?

8)   What request did the servant turn down by the family? Ultimately, who was made to

        choose their fate and what was their decision?

Genesis 24:54-58

9)   What happened after Rebekah was sent away?

Genesis 24:59-67

10)   Read over **Genesis 25:1-6**. How did Abraham treat his children and who was given

        the most? What else did Abraham have (verse 6)?

11)   How old was Abraham when he died and what did his two oldest sons (Ishmael and

        Isaac) do with his body?

Genesis 25:7-10

Genesis 25:11-18 describes the blessing of Isaac and the lineage of Ishmael. Look at verse 17 and notice how old Ishmael was when he died and verse 16 and how many sons he had. There will be a similarity with the number of sons with one of Isaac's son's Jacob and his children later on.

PERSONAL STUDY

A)   The servant's prayer was very specific. What can we learn from this and how prayer can be tailored?

B)   Although this prayer was specific, sometimes we shouldn't be so detail. When is this and why would you have time when you can be detailed?

C)   Rebekah showed herself to have great hospitality, which is a sign of great character. Describe why this is a good quality for a spouse, parent, and person?

D)   When looking for a spouse what character traits should we look for?

E)   Abraham wanted his son to marry from his kindred or like believers. Why is this important in their time as well as now to share someone with a similar value system?

LESSON 14

Genesis 25:19 – 26

Like Father, Like Son

1)   How old was Isaac when he got married and what did he ask God?

Genesis 25:19-21

2)   Rebekah could feel a struggle in her stomach and asked God for an answer. What

        was God's response and what prophecy was given to her?

Genesis 25:22-24

3)   Describe the two sons. How where they different from one another? Who gravitated

        to which parent?

Genesis 25:25-28

4)   What mistake did the eldest brother, Esau, make?

Genesis 25:29-34, Hebrews 12:16-17

5)   What promise did God make to Isaac? Where did the Lord tell him to go?

Genesis 26:1-5

6)   Isaac committed the exact same error as his dad. What was it and how is this representative of parent problems and faults being passed down to their children?

Genesis 26:6-7

7)   How did Abimelch find out the truth? What order was given by the King?

Genesis 26:8-11

8)   Isaac was blessed by God but was in contention with the residents of Gerar (Genesis

26:12-21). Where did Isaac go and what promise did God reiterate?

Genesis 26:22-25

9)   What happened between Abimlech and Isaac? Why was this important for the future

generations of the two people?

Genesis 26:26-33

10)   What mistake did Esau do? How did his parents respond?

Genesis 26:34-35

PERSONAL STUDY

A)   Rebekah received notice from God that the younger son would be great. Do you

think this influenced her behavior and treatment of the two sons? If you knew, one

child would be greater then the other, would you show favor to one child?

B)   Jacob asked Esau for his birthright. It was as if he knew he was to be great. Although

Jacob was securing a promise made by God, would the Lord operate like this? Do we

as people force situations because we believe we're doing God's will?

C)   Isaac made the exact same mistake as his dad by claiming his wife as his sibling.

Unlike his dad, he was not Rebekah's brother at all, which means he completely lied.

This act was done after God had promised a major blessing. Why do we fear people

more then we respect and obey God?

D)   The Lord blessed Isaac no matter where he went. How can we be blessed and bless

those around us?

LESSON 15

Genesis 27 – 28

It's All Part Of The Plan

1)   Isaac was getting old and desired to bless his son. Whom did Isaac desire to bless

and what mission did he give him?

Genesis 27:1-4

2)   Rebekah over heard the request and devised a plan of her own. She remembered

God's promise (Genesis 25:23), and decided to fulfill that by her own doing. What

was her plan for Jacob?

Genesis 27:5-12

3)   Read **Genesis 27:13-17** and describe what Rebekah did to enact her plan? Would

tricking her husband be the means that God set forth?

4)   Jacob who is now falsely setting himself up as Esau is now with his dad. What happened during the ceremony that Jacob is almost caught? What does he say to convince his father that he is Esau?

Genesis 27:18-22

5)   What is the blessing that Isaac gave to Jacob?

Genesis 27:23-29

6)   What happened as soon as Jacob left? How did Esau respond and what blessing did he receive?

Genesis 27:30-40

7)   Jacob took Esau's birthright and stole his blessing. What was Esau's reaction to his younger brother and what did Rebekah order Jacob to do?

Genesis 27:41-46

8)   Isaac formally blessed Jacob after he had been deceived what was said in the blessing and what request did Isaac have for his son?

Genesis 28:1-5

9)   Esau lost his birthright and blessing. However, he still desired the love and approval from his parents. What did Esau do to try to please his parents?

Genesis 28:6-9

10)   While traveling to Padanaran, Jacob stopped and had a dream. Describe the dream and God's promise.

Genesis 28:10-19

11)   What was Jacob's response to the dream?

Genesis 28:20-22

PERSONAL STUDY

A)   If you where in Esau's place, how would you react to your brother after stealing your

        birthright and blessing? Should Esau take some of the blame?

B)   Jacob used God as a means of stating why he was able to get the food. Are there

        times when we attribute blessings to God, although we know that the Lord had

        nothing to do with it?

C)   Why would the Lord bless Jacob with the blessing compare to Esau? Review both

      men and their behavior. Is there something that Esau did that would not sit well with

      God?

D)   Are we like Rebekah who manipulated a situation to force what she believes is

      God's plan? Why are we eager to do this? Could the Lord have worked out another

      means to bless Jacob and is there anything you're doing currently that is not

      according to God's will although you knew it would help His call in your life?

LESSON 16

Genesis 29 – 30:25

The Family Of Jacob

1)   Jacob sought out looking for his wife amongst his mother's family, (Genesis 29:1-5).

         After finding the right people who did Jacob see and what did he do?

Genesis 29:6-10

2)   Jacob lived with Laban for a month, (Genesis 29:11-14), before giving Jacob a job.

         What was the wages agreed upon between the two men?

Genesis 29:15-19

3)   Describe the two daughters of Laban, what difference is made between the two?

Genesis 29:17

4)   Read the following scripture **Genesis 29:20-25**, what payment was Jacob supposed

         to get and what did he receive?

5)   What tradition did Laban use to get more service out of Jacob? Remembering that

Laban and Rebekah are siblings, can you see a similar trait between the two?

Genesis 29:26-29

6)   How did Jacob feel about his two wives and what did the Lord do in the family?

Genesis 29:30-31

7)   What are the first four children of Leah and why did she name each of them?

Genesis 29:32-35

A_____

_____

B_____

_____

C_____

_____

D_____

_____

8)   How did Rachel feel about Leah's amount of children? What was the solution what

did she name the sons?

Genesis 30:1-6

A_____

_____

B_____

_____

9)   Not to be out done by her sister, Leah set up a plan of her own. What was it and what

did she name the children and why?

Genesis 30:9-13

A_____

_____

B_____

_____

10)   How far did the rivalry go between the two sisters? What form of barter did they use

for Jacob's attention? What children came out of that?

Genesis 30:14-21

      A_____

_____

      B_____

_____

      C_____

_____

11)   What blessing finally came to Rachel?

Genesis 30:22-24

PERSONAL STUDY

A)   Jacob clearly loved Rachel. However, he was duped into marrying Leah. If in his

      place, would you treat the two wives differently then him? What advice would you

      give Jacob?

B)   Why would God close the womb of Rachel compare to her sister?

C)   Leah is clearly unloved by her husband. This is a horrible situation for any spouse.

      Leah believed that because of the custom at that time, having sons would bring

      happiness in her marriage. If you were Leah, what would you do to bring love and

      joy into your marriage? Especially when you know, your spouse is in love with

      someone else?

D)   Jacob worked hard to get Rachel (14 years of service). To him it was worth it because he loved her. Looks alone could not have drawn Jacob to do hard labor. What was it about Rachel that made him love her so much? Can a love like that be obtained in today's society? If so how?

E)   Zilpah and Bilhah where the two handmaids used as weapons in a sister's feud. They had children but didn't get the chance to name them. How where they feeling during this time and can we use people today for our own good? How should we treat all people regardless of class, race, gender, and social situation?

LESSON 17

Genesis 30:25 – 31

Jacob's Flight Back Home

1)   Jacob desires to have his own place and go back home. What reason did Laban give

him to stay?

Genesis 30:25-27

2)   What wages was worked out between Jacob and Laban before leaving?

Genesis 30:28-34

3)   What did Laban do to try to steal Jacob's livestock? How did Jacob get him back and

become a success?

Genesis 30:35-43

4)   What problem occurred in Laban's camp and what call did Jacob get from God?

Genesis 31:1-3

5)   Jacob consulted with his wives before leaving. Describe the dream that God give to

Jacob. What where the wives response to how their dad behaved?

Genesis 31:4-16

6)   Someone in Jacob's family took something of Laban's. What was it and who did the

crime?

Genesis 31:17-21

7)   Laban found out about Jacob leaving and his idols that where missing. He pursued

      and God came to him in a dream. Describe the dream and message for Laban. How

      did Laban treat Jacob once he met him? What did he want to get back?

Genesis 31:22-30

8)   What reason did Jacob give for leaving? Had he known that someone took the idols

      would he have made such a bold statement?

Genesis 31:31-35

9)   Jacob was furious when the items where not found in the camp, (Genesis 31:36-43).

      Nevertheless, the two men made a covenant between one another to squash any bad

      feelings. Describe the covenant and its importance.

Genesis 31:44-55

PERSONAL STUDY

A)   God showed Jacob the means to overcome Laban's trickery. Jacob listens and was blessed. Why is obedience so important in receiving a blessing from God?

B)   No different then Isaac, Jacob blessed those around him do to his relationship with God. In what ways are people being blessed because of your relationship with God?

C)   God intervenes on Jacob's behalf by telling Laban not to speak rough to him. This is an example of seeing God work things out even when we don't know it. How has God protected us from unseen danger? List ways God shows compassion, love, and mercy in your life?

D)   Rachel taking Laban's idols revealed something about her character. What does this

      say about her relationship with God? Why would she take these things?

E)   Did Laban have a right to be mad over what happened with his daughters being

      swept away and his idols stolen? How would you respond if placed in his situation?

LESSON 18

Genesis 32 – 33

From Jacob To Israel

1)   What message did Jacob send to Esau to help make peace?

Genesis 32:1-5

2)   Jacob was frightened over the possibility of meeting Esau because of the past and his army of 400 men, (Genesis 32:6-8). Read Jacob's prayer to God. What is the base of his prayer and how is he showing humility? What can we take personally in our prayer life as an example?

Genesis 32:9-12

3)   What plan did Jacob come up with upon meeting his brother?

Genesis 32:13-20

4)   What event happened when Jacob was by himself and how did this change him and
        his family forever?

Genesis 32:24-32, Hosea 12:2-4

5)   How did Jacob divide the family before meeting Esau? Does this reveal a hierarchy
        of love for the various wives, handmaids, and their children?

Genesis 33:1-2

6)   Jacob (Israel) was showing himself humble before his brother at the fear of death.
        Esau could have gotten revenge for his brother deception many years ago. How did
        Esau respond to his brother?

Genesis 33:3-9

7)   What request did Jacob make to Esau? What happened after the two men left?

Genesis 33:10-20

PERSONAL STUDY

A)   Jacob wrestled with an angel even when his thigh was injured because he desired a

        blessing from God. When it comes to our blessings (spiritual, family, health, money,

        mental strength, etc) and life gets tough, should we leave God or continue with Him

        in faith and prayer knowing that He has great things in store for us?

B)   What are ways to grown with God and use the blessings He has already provided for

        you to help others?

C)   Jacob's name was changed to Israel, much like his grandfather's name was changed.

Why would a change be necessary for Jacob/Israel to enter a new station in his life?

What changes will God have to make in your character?

D)   Esau greets Jacob with love. In our lives we might have wronged someone or they

could have done us wrong. How can we use Esau's forgiveness as an example in

how we should forgive others? Is it easy to forgive? What steps should we take to

genuinely forgive someone who has hurt us?

LESSON 19

Vengeance And Pain

Genesis 34 – 36

1)   What happened to Dinah?

Genesis 34:1-4

2)   Describe the reaction from both families? Was Jacob's sons justified in their anger?

Genesis 34:5-10

3)   Shechem, prince of the land, desired to give anything to marry Dinah. What request

        was made of Schechem and the men in his group?

Genesis 34:11-17

4)   How did Hamor and Schechem respond to the request? Look at verse 21 and state

        how Jacob and his sons where described in their eyes? What other blessings did the

        men see by joining with Jacob family?

Genesis 34:18-23

5)   What event happened after the circumcision? How did Jacob respond to his sons,

        Simeon and Levi's?

Genesis 34:24-31

6)   Jacob was to get his family on one accord. What where they suppose to do and where

        were they suppose to go?

Genesis 35:1-8

7)   God came to Jacob when he built an alter as requested. What did God say and how

        was this confirmation from the wrestling even earlier in Jacob's life?

Genesis 35:9-15

8)   What tragic event happened to the family?

Genesis 35:16-21

9)   Next to each name list what sons where born to the mother. There should be 12.

Genesis 35:23 – Leah

_____

_____

Genesis 35:24 – Rachel

_____

_____

Genesis 35:25 – Bilhah

_____

_____

Genesis 35:26 – Zilpah

_____

_____

10)   Isaac lived a long time and died at the age of 180. Besides Jacob who else came to be

        a part of the funeral ceremony?

Genesis 35:27-29

Chapter 36 is the lineage of Esau. This is important because it helps us with connecting

people and tribes as the Israelites maneuver to the promise land (Exodus – Joshua). You will

notice that Esau is also referred to as Edom in which he became father of the Edomites.

PERSONAL STUDY

A)   God had Jacob/Israel family to put away foreign gods and worship Him. Why would

        the Lord desire to establish this?

B)   How can Jacob's non-response lead his son to the slayings against Schechem and

        men of his community? If you were in Jacob's situation, what would you do

        differently so your children would not take revenge?

C)   The sons of Jacob lied to the men of Hamor. How can a lie start up problems in your

        area? As Christians, by caring Christ name what happened when we misrepresent

        God? Why is a lie in our behavior, character or words dangers to those we are

        ministering to?

D)   Benjamin's name was Benoni until Jacob changed it. Why would he do this and how

        important is a name? Do we in our current society take the time to research and make

        sure that our baby's name means something?

E)   Reuben committed a serious wrong by sleeping with Bilhah. How can this bring

        confusion in the family? What problem can happen today if we began to have

        inappropriate relationships with family rather by blood or marriage?

LESSON 20

Genesis 38

Judah And Tamar

Chapter 38 goes into the life of Judah. At first, this would seem odd because the Bible does not go into detail on the other sons of Jacob except Joseph. However, when you read Matthew 1:1-16 you will see a connection between Judah and the lineage of Jesus Christ.

1)   Judah saw a Canaanite woman and had children with her. What was her name and the three sons that came from their union?

Genesis 38:1-5

2)   Tamar was given to Judah's first son as a wife. What happened to him and the second son of Judah?

Genesis 38:6-10

3)   What promise did Judah make to Tamar?

Genesis 38:11

4)   Tamar was tired of waiting for Judah so she took action to fulfill his promise. What

         did she do?

Genesis 38:12-14

5)   Who did Judah think Tamar was and what did he give her as a down payment?

Genesis 38:15-18

6)   Judah came back to the place with the official payment. Did he find the woman he

         was looking for?

Genesis 38:19-23

7)   When Judah found out that Tamar was pregnant he was furious, but what fact did she

         reveal quieted his anger? What where the names of the children?

Genesis 38:24-30

PERSONAL STUDY

A)   When we think of Christ, it's hard to imagine Judah and Tamar's "relationship" being a part of His lineage. What does this example state of Christ involving all people into his family? Is there anything too hard for God to save you from?

B)   Judah openly slept with a woman he thought was a prostitute then was going to give her food as payment. Do we sometimes treat relationships in a "prostitute" type of way? Meaning, do we give each other food or gifts in hopes of carnal pleasure?

C)   Onan did not want to impregnate Tamar because that was his brother's wife. However, Er was dead so it was Onan's responsibility to take over. Why would Onan not wanting to have a child with Tamar get him killed? Remember that he "knew" her but choose not to get her pregnant.

LESSON 21

Genesis 37 & 39

The Dreamer

1)   Describe Joseph's relationship with his brothers. Why was it that way?

Genesis 37:1-4

2)   Joseph had two dreams. Describe both and the family's reaction to them.

Genesis 37:5-11

3)   Joseph was sent by his father to find his brothers. He came across someone who told him they where in Dothan and while he approached them what where their thoughts? What plan of action was ultimately set up to help save Joseph and why?

Genesis 37:18-22

4)   One of the brothers had an idea to make profit from Joseph. Who was he and what

        happened when Reuben returned?

Genesis 37:23-36

5)   Describe Joseph's life in Egypt? How was it evident that God was with him?

Genesis 39:1-6

6)   What temptation did Joseph fight? What reason did he state to not give in?

Genesis 39:7-10

7)   What happened to Joseph although he was innocent?

Genesis 39:11-20

8)   What was Joseph's standing in prison?

Genesis 39:21-23

PERSONAL STUDY

A)   Joseph freely told his family his dreams. This ended up causing more strife and
        jealousy to brew toward him. Are their times when God wants us to keep quiet on
        some of the things He has shared with you? Like Joseph, can we cause other people
        to have the same reaction when we share too much information?

B)   Reuben believed the situation was under control but things did not go according to
        plan. List times when we handle things only to have them go wrong.

C)   Joseph believed that his sin not only affected his boss but God as well. When we are disobeying God, how will our actions affect both God and people? Why is it important for our character to be in line with God and obeying His word?

D)   Potipher's wife is a good representation of how sin and temptation can be relentless and come after you daily. However, like Joseph we can be strong and overcome these temptations. What issues are you dealing with that is a strong temptation and problem in your life?

LESSON 22

Genesis 40 – 41

The Rise Of Joseph

1.)   Who was thrown into the same prison area as Joseph?

Genesis 40:1-4

2.)   The butler and baker had troubling dreams. Before listening to their dreams, who does Joseph give credit for the interpretation of their vision.

Genesis 40:5-8

3.)   What was the butler's dream and how did Joseph interpret it? How would the butler's dream help Joseph?

Genesis 40:9-15

4.)   What was the baker's dream? How would you have responded if you heard such a

        dream forecast to you?

Genesis 40:16-19

5.)   Where the interpretations of the dream correct? Did the baker help Joseph?

Genesis 40:20-23

6.)   After two years of the Butler's release the Pharaoh had two disturbing dreams.

        Describe both of them.

Genesis 41:1-7

7.)   Since nobody in Pharaoh's group could interpret the dream, how did Joseph's name

        get mention as a dream interpreter? What did they do to Joseph to prepare him to

        meet the Pharaoh?

Genesis 41:8-14

8.)   Like once before, who does Joseph give credit for the interpretation of the dream?

Genesis 41:15-16

9.)   Pharaoh told Joseph his dream, (Genesis 41:17-24). What was the interpretation of

Pharaoh's dream and what was the solution to the problem?

Genesis 41:25-36

10.)   List some of the things that Joseph gained after he interpreted the dream.

Genesis 41:37-45

A.   _____

B.   _____

C.   _____

D.   _____

E.   _____

11.)   How old was Joseph when he interpreted the Pharaoh's dream? Describe life in Egypt during the seven plenty and drought years.

Genesis 41:46-57

PERSONAL STUDY

A.)   Notice how Joseph gave God the credit for his abilities. With our talents, skills,

        abilities, and blessings why is it important for us to give God the credit?

B.)   How could a person comfort the baker after hearing his dream? What response do

        you believe that the baker gave to Joseph after hearing his dream interpreted?

C.)   Joseph was in a prison cell, when he was brought before the Pharaoh. He had no idea that a dreamed was dream and that it would be years later when the butler would remember him. However, God did not forget Joseph and the Hebrew servant were blessed immediately. How does this section of the story give you hope in your life with regards to blessings and being able to move up to serve God? Notice that Joseph was blessed so that he could minister to an entire nation and those surrounding Egypt. How are God blessings able to help you to bless others?

D.)   After waiting for two years Joseph could have given up when the Butler left the prison. However, he didn't and God was able to use him to do great things. Are you waiting for anything to come through? Remember that it takes patience to wait and depend on God. Pray on what you're waiting for and know that God will bless you with that promise.

E)   Compare Joseph in Lesson 21 to this one. What lesson did Joseph learn and character change did he go through to be of use for God? What things are you learning and how can you overcome these issues to be a better person for God?

LESSON 23

Genesis 42 – 43

Joseph's Family Arrives

1)   Israel sent his sons to go and get food for the family. Who did not go and why?

Genesis 42:1-4

2)   When 10 of Joseph's brothers arrived in Egypt, what did he accuse them of and what did he do to them? Why did Joseph treat his brothers in this manner?

Genesis 42:5-17

3)   What command did Joseph give to his brothers, and which brother had to stay behind?

Genesis 42:18-24

4)   What surprise did Joseph's older brothers find when they got home?

Genesis 42:25-28

5)   The brothers tried to explain to Israel what happened to them and Simeon. What vow

did Reuben state, to make sure Benjamin would be okay? What was Israel's

decision?

Genesis 42:29-38

6)   Which son convinced Israel to bring Benjamin to Egypt with them on their trip to get

more food? What arguments did he use to convince his father?

Genesis 43:1-10

7)   When Israel's sons returned a second time to Egypt, what did they bring and who

was with them?

Genesis 43:11-15

8)   Upon seeing Benjamin with his brothers, what did Joseph do for his family? What

        reasoning did the brothers feel they where meeting with Joseph and how did they

        explain themselves?

Genesis 43:16-25

9)   Notice what happens between Joseph and his brothers. What dream does this

        confirm? How did Joseph respond when seeing his family?

Genesis 43:27-32, Genesis 37:5-8

10)   What did Joseph do that could have revealed who he was to his brothers?

Genesis 43:33-34

PERSONAL STUDY

A)   No matter how unlikely it may seem, a vision or prophetic word from God always

        come through. When Joseph told his brothers about the wheat bowing down, it

        seemed impossible at the time. However, years later, it happens. Think about your

        life and God's promises. Are you certain that what God has spoken in your life will

        happen? Write down at least one thing you are sure of that will happen because God

        said it.

B)   When Israel refused to allow Benjamin to leave and Simeon to be in prison, was he

        showing favoritism amongst the brothers? Could some of his animosity come from

        when Simeon killed a village worth of men? (Genesis 34)

C)   Where is Israel's behavior of showing favoritism between his sons coming from?

      What ways can we show the same behavior to our children, employees, or friends?

D)   The brothers where faced with a dilemma when having their money returned. For them, this was done on purpose, however, we might get extra money and know it was a mistake. For example, if a bank teller counting out to much money; or the wrong change given to you in a grocery store. What are we suppose to do in a situation like this? Why is this show of good character and representing Christ to the world?

LESSON 24

Genesis 44 – 45

The Reveal

1)   What mission did Joseph give his steward?

Genesis 44:1-16

2)   What is the response of the brothers?

Genesis 44:7-11

3)   When the cup is found in Benjamin's bag, what is his punishment? What did Joseph

do with the other brothers?

Genesis 44:12-17

4)   Which brother came up in defense of Benjamin? List some of the arguments he gave

for saving Benjamin's life and what was he willing to do to save his youngest

brother's life?

Genesis 44:18-34

5)   Describe Joseph's reaction to Judah's plea?

Genesis 45:1-4

6)   Name three reasons why God sent Joseph into Egypt?

Genesis 45:5-8

A)

B)

C)

7) What was Joseph's request for his brothers?

Genesis 45:9-15

8) How did Pharaoh respond to the knowledge of Joseph's family being in town?

Genesis 45:16–24

9) How did Israel respond to the news of Joseph being alive?

Genesis 45:25-28

PERSONAL STUDY

A)   Look over the reasons that Joseph gives for God sending him into Egypt (Genesis 45:5-8). How was the nation blessed due to Joseph's position?

B)   If you where Joseph and you had a life of a farmer to being sold as a slave, to being elevated as the top man in the household, then to prison, to being in the King's court, would you view the hardships as worth it? Why was it necessary for Joseph to learn through the trials?

C)   We see parts of Judah's character when he was willing to offer himself in place of his brother Benjamin. What about him, could have made the Lord come through his seed instead of the others?

D)   Like Judah showed love, is there anyone you would be willing to become a substitute

for their pain? Think about how hard that is and write down the things you've done,

been through, and how Christ has been your substitute.

E)   Was Joseph right for treating his brothers the way he did by accusing them of being

spies and placing the silver cup in their bag? What reasons could Joseph of done

this? If given the opportunity, would you treat people you love who have wronged

you the same way as Joseph treated his brothers?

LESSON 25

Genesis 46 – 47

What Once Was Lost Is Now Found

1)   God came to comfort and reassure Israel of his trip into Egypt. Summarize the words

that God said to Jacob?

Genesis 46:1-4

Read Genesis 46:5-26. This will give a description of who went to Egypt from Israel's

family. Notice the amount of children for each son. At the end, there is a total count for

people going.

2)   Why did Israel and his family have to dwell in the land of Goshen?

Genesis 46:31-34

3)   What request did Joseph's family make to Pharaoh, what was his response?

Genesis 47:1-6

4)   Upon meeting the Pharaoh, what did Israel do for the King?

Genesis 47:7-10

5)   Describe the famine and the various remedies that Joseph had for the people.

Genesis 47:11-26

6)   What promise did Israel have Joseph to make?

Genesis 47:27-31

PERSONAL STUDY

A)   Before he left God came to Israel to comfort him. Describe in your life the times
      where God came and gave you comfort and knowledge when he was with you
      through all your changes. These changes can be marriage, a new job, children,
      school, new church, or any other event.

B)   Look at how many people where traveling with Israel. God promised a blessing in
      the multitude of people from Abraham's line. How is this fulfilling of the prophecy
      give you peace for the future fulfillment of promises in your life?

C)   Even though Pharaoh did not believe in the same God as Israel, how is Israel's showing of respect an example to when dealing with people regardless of their personal beliefs?

D)   Joseph constantly had idea to help the land with the famine crisis. In times of despair, how can God use His people to bring hope and solutions to the problems of the world?

E)   Why was it important for Israel to be buried with his family?

LESSON 26

Genesis 48 – 50

The End Of The Beginning

1.)   Israel knew his time was short and wanted to start blessing his sons. Before the other

11, Israel had a private session with Joseph. Not only did he promise blessings to

Joseph, but who else in Joseph's family did Israel bless?

Genesis 48:1-10

2.)   Where did Joseph place his two sons by Israel for the blessing?

Genesis 48:11-13

3)   Did Israel bless the youth according to birth order or according to God's direction?

What lessons from his own life did he learn that influenced this decision?

Genesis 48:14-22

4.)   Israel passes down blessings and a foretelling of what each son will become. Next to
        the name write down the blessing/curse/foretelling of each son. All of the blessings
        are found in Genesis 49.

Reuben :3-4

Levi and Simeon :5-7

Judah :8-12

Zebulun :13

Issachar :14-15

Dan :16-18

Gad :19

Asher :20

Naphtali :21

Joseph :22-26

Benjamin :27

5.)   What was the last request from Israel to his sons?

Genesis 49:28-33

6.)   What act did they do to the body of a dead person, that we still do to this day and how long did they mourn for Israel's death?

Genesis 50:1-3

7.)   What request did Joseph ask of Pharaoh?

Genesis 50:4-6

8.)   After they buried their father (Genesis 50:7-14) what was the reaction of the 11 brothers toward Joseph? How did he calm their fears?

Genesis 50:15-21

9.)   Like his father before him, what request did Joseph make about his own death? How old was Joseph when he died?

Genesis 50:22-26

PERSONAL STUDY

A)   The blessings that where handed down to the 12 sons where based on who the

       children where and not tied to birth order. What lessons can we learn from traditions

       of society and what God has ordained or informed us to do?

B)   Describe how your reactions in life can affect the blessings that God has in store for

       you.

C)   What means can you take to inherit those blessings by living in the will of God and

       not just the desires of society?

D)   We see in Israel and Joseph, that both wanted to be buried in their homeland. How

can culture and our connection to the past, help guide us today and into the future?

E)   What people from the book of Genesis do you relate to and see yourself going

through a similar situation? Did the means that they handled a situation help teach

you how to or not treat the problem in a similar fashion?

F)   For the entire book of Genesis, what lessons did you learn and can apply to your life?

Closing Thought

Remember that God has great things in store for you. Some of us are already in that framework of life, but some still desire to get there. There's not one person who is born, that the Lord does not have an important work for you to accomplish. Some people chose to do it others do not.

Be the person who will, inquire to God, "Why am I here?" Genesis is the foundation for all humanity and spiritual references for the Bible. In your life, start up a foundation in God, not only for yourself, but for all people you will encounter, as well as your children if you have any.

The ultimate quest is to see Jesus in Heaven. The ultimate question is "What must I do, to commune with Jesus?" When God responds in your life, then it's up to you to follow Him or continue to be in bondage to the ways of the world.

A Brief Outline on the Book of Genesis

Creation   **Genesis 1 - 2**
The account of the beginning is told in two chapters for a rounded view of the beginnings of the world. These two chapters help provide a picture of God forming everything around us and for all people.

The First Sin   **Genesis 3**
Something as simple as eating fruit is what led to the proliferation of sin throughout the world. Here is where we find the origins of sin and how all evil thoughts and actions have its beginnings in trying to be God.

The First Murder   **Genesis 4:1–15**
Cain was jealous so he slew his brother Abel. When in reality, had he listen to the Lord the hatred he had for his brother would have been non-existent.

Genealogy of People   **Genesis 4:16 – 6:4**
Here you will find the line of Cain and Seth, the son who replaced Abel. We here names like Methuselah the man who is recorded to live the longest at 969 years, Lamech, Enoch, and the start of Noah.

Noah and the Flood   **Genesis 6:5 – 7:23**
God flooded the entire earth to wash it of its iniquity but spared Noah and his family. Here is where we learn of the Ark that was built and the miracle of getting animals unto the boat.

Noah and his Family   **Genesis 8 – 9**
We learn that everything wasn't so perfect after the flood but we also learn about Noah and his three sons.

Genealogy of Noah   **Genesis 10**
This chapter goes into detail about Noah's three sons and how their families where the start of future tribes/cities/and people. Not only are Japheth, Ham, and Shem mentioned but also so is Canaan, Ham's son.

Tower of Babel   **Genesis 11:1-9**
God ordered the people to spread out and that the world will never be destroyed by water. However, they choose to stay in one spot and build a tower to escape another possible flood. So God confused their languages to force them to populate the world.

Abraham   **Genesis 11:10 – 12:20**
This chapter is the start of Abraham and the covenant God had with him. Also in this section, Abraham was scared he would lose his life so he told the men that Sarah was his sister instead of his wife.

Abraham and Lot   **Genesis 13 - 14**
Lot and Abraham separated and while Lot was in Sodom, an enemy kidnapped him and the people of the city. Abraham goes in with his servants and save Lot and the rest of the Sodomites.

The promise of a child   **Genesis 15**
God comes to Abraham and promises a child again.

Ishmael comes from Hagar   **Genesis 16**
Out of impatience, Sarah suggests to Abraham that he has a child with her handmaid Hagar. He goes with the plan and has Ishmael, which causes strife in the household.

Institution of Circumcision   **Genesis 17**
Abraham name changes from Abram to Abraham, as well as Sarai to Sarah. Also in this chapter, we have the institution of circumcision as a covenant between God and his people.

Visit from two angels   **Genesis 18**
Abraham gets a visit from two angels, taking the form as men, stating to him that they would have a child within a year. Sarah doesn't believe and is caught in a lie. Abraham also convinces the men not to destroy Sodom if 10 righteous people are within its gates.

Destruction of the Twin Cities   **Genesis 19**
We see a glimpse of the problems within Sodom as well as how that culture affected Lot's family.

Birth of Isaac   **Genesis 20 – 21**
Once again, Abraham lied about his marriage to Sarah and Isaac was born.

Abraham's sacrifice   **Genesis 22 - 23**
God called Abraham to sacrifice Isaac. He had to have faith in God to know that his Lord knew what was best since this was the chosen child. Sarah dies and Abraham is able to buy land so his heirs can have a claim to the land.

Isaac's wife and death of Abraham   **Genesis 24 – 25:18**

Abraham sends his top servant to find Isaac a wife. He was able to find Rebekah at the well giving his camels water. Also in this section, Abraham remarries, have more children and dies.

Twins are born, Isaac lies   **Genesis 25:19 – 26:35**

Isaac and Rebekah are blessed with twins, Esau and Jacob. God informs Rachel of twins. She learns that the youngest would rule the older. A taste of this shows up when Jacob gets Esau to sell his birthright for a pot of food. Also in this section, Isaac repeats Abraham sin of lying about his marriage to Rebekah.

Jacob takes the Blessing   **Genesis 27**

Jacob, with the help of Rebekah, tricks Isaac and takes Esau's blessing. Esau is clearly unhappy and vows to kill Jacob.

Jacob flees and his dream   **Genesis 28**

Jacob has to leave his home. He would never see his mother again. Before his trip, Isaac blesses his properly. On his flight to Padanaram, Jacob has a dream and vowed a vow with God.

Jacob labors for Rachel   **Genesis 29:1-30**

Jacob works for 14 years to have the honor in marrying Rachel. During this time, he was tricked by his uncle and for the first 7 years of hard work, he had to marry Leah.

List of Jacob's first 11 sons   **Genesis 29:31 – 30:25**

Here is the list of Jacob's 11 sons, who their mother where, and the reason behind their names.

Jacob leaves to go home   **Genesis 30:26 – 31:55**

Jacob outsmarts Laban to have the better livestock and sneaks out with his family. Laban catches him, and they decide to make a covenant between one another.

Wrestling with an angel   **Genesis 32**

Jacob hears news of Esau coming to meet him and is nervous. During a time of being by himself, he wrestles with an angel until he is blessed. Jacob name changes to Israel by God.

Peace between brothers   **Genesis 33**

Esau and Israel makes peace with one another.

Revenge for the defilement of Dinah   **Genesis 34**
Levi and Simeon enact revenge for Dinah, because an area man has raped her and decide to
marry their sister. Jacob is displeased because now the family is a marked target for other
groups due to their anger.

Death of Isaac and Rachel   **Genesis 35**
God establishes a covenant with Israel at Bethel. Also in this chapter, Rachel and Isaac die.

Genealogy of Esau   **Genesis 36**
We learn the history of Esau and the Dukes that would come from him.

Joseph sold into slavery   **Genesis 37**
Israel loved Joseph the most. He showed it and made the man a marked target from his older
brothers. Joseph has a talent for interpreting dreams, which fuels even more jealousy against
him. While searching for his brothers, Joseph is thrown into a pit and sold into slavery.

Judah and his child with Temar   **Genesis 38**
Judah has a child with Temar, the woman who was suppose to have his grandchild, not son.
The line of Christ comes from her oldest child Pharez.

Joseph thrown into prison   **Genesis 39**
Joseph is thrown into prison because Potiphar's wife lied and said he tried to rape her but in
reality he ran from the temptation. This chapter shows how no matter where Joseph goes,
God always blessed him. While a slave to even a prisoner.

Joseph interrupts dreams in prison   **Genesis 40**
While in prison, Joseph interrupts the dreams for the Baker and Butler. He believed that he
would be leaving the prison soon however it was not time.

From prisoner to the King's Court   **Genesis 41**
Joseph is taken out of prison two years later when Pharaoh finds out that he can interrupt
dreams. Joseph gives God the credit and not only interrupts the dream but give a solution for
the drought that was going to happen.

Joseph sees his brothers   **Genesis 42**
Joseph does not reveal to his brothers his identity and desires to see Benjamin. He holds
Simeon there until they return with the youngest son. He is testing them to see if they have
changed.

More Tests   **Genesis 43 – 44**

Joseph tests his brothers to see if they're jealous if Benjamin is treated better as well as their love for him if he is to die.

Joseph reveals himself   **Genesis 45**

Joseph shows his brothers who he really is, and that he is alive. They celebrate and Joseph desires for them to move to Egypt as well as Israel his father.

Life in Egypt   **Genesis 46 - 47**

Here we see life in Egypt for Israel and his family with Joseph. These chapters go into the customs of the Egyptians as well as life during a drought.

The blessings and death of Israel   **Genesis 48 – 50:14**

Israel blesses Joseph's sons Ephraim and Manasseh. Then he blesses each of his own sons as well foretell of what will become of their future. Israel dies and his taken home to be buried.

Joseph dies   **Genesis 50:15-26**

Joseph's brothers are worried that Joseph will enact revenge against them, but he assures them that he has no malice in his heart. Joseph dies, but gets the family to promise to bury him in his homeland when they can.

Main Characters from the book of Genesis

Name	Chapters	Brief Info
Abel	4	listen to God and was murdered by his brother Cain
Abimelech	20, 26	the king Abraham and Isaac lies to
Abraham	11 - 25	became the father for 3 different religions
Adam	1 - 4	the first man of the world
Cain	4	the first murderer
Dinah	34	she was defiled which led her brothers to kill in retribution
Esau	25 - 36	Jacob's twin brother who did not take his birthright/blessing seriously
Eve	1 - 4	the first woman of the world
Hagar	16 - 21	Ishmael's mother
Isaac	21 - 28, 35	Abraham's promised child
Ishmael	16 - 25	the child of Abraham's impatience
Jacob/Israel	25 - 49	the man who had 12 sons which later formed a nation
Joseph	30 - 50	one of the sons who was able to save his family and entire region
Judah	29 - 50	Christ comes through his line, has own chapter in 38
Laban	29	Israel's uncle who tricks him to get more work and weaker animals
Laban	24, 29 - 31	Rebekah's brother, who gives Jacob his two daughters for wives
Leah	29 - 37	the wife of Israel who was unloved
Lot	12 - 14, 19	Abraham's nephew who followed him until Sodom
Noah	5 - 9	God saved him from the flood
Pharaoh	40 - 50	the King of Egypt during Joseph time who showed him kindness
Rachel	29 - 35	the wife of Israel who was loved
Rebekah	24 - 27	Israel's mother who loved her youngest more then Esau
Sarah	11 - 23	Abraham's first wife, and mother to Isaac
Seth	4 - 5	God used his line to replace Abel's
Temar	38	Had a child by Judah

12 Children of Israel

Below is a list of the twelve children from Israel. Although when you look up the actual tribe it's a little different then what's listed, since Levi, became a priestly tribe and two of the tribes are named after Joseph's children.

Dinah was another important child, born from Leah. She comes up later in the story involving some revenge by her two brothers Simeon and Levi.

Son Name	Mom's Name	Wife or Handmaid	Meaning of Name	Scripture
Reuben	Leah	Wife	Son	Genesis 29:32
Simeon	Leah	Wife	Unloved	Genesis 29:33
Levi	Leah	Wife	Become Attached	Genesis 29:34
Judah	Leah	Wife	Praise	Genesis 29:35
Dan	Bilhah	Handmaid (Rachel)	Judge	Genesis 30:6
Naphtali	Bilhah	Handmaid (Rachel)	My Wrestling	Genesis 30:8
Gad	Zilpah	Handmaid (Leah)	Fortune	Genesis 30:11
Asher	Zilpah	Handmaid (Leah)	Happy	Genesis 30:13
Issachar	Leah	Wife	Hire	Genesis 30:18
Zebulun	Leah	Wife	Endowment	Genesis 30:20
Joseph	Rachel	Wife	He Will Add	Genesis 30:25
Benjamin	Rachel	Wife	Son of Right Hand	Genesis 35:18

10037353R00083

Made in the USA
Lexington, KY
17 September 2018